The Ultimate Guide to Entrepreneurship

Surendra Sahu

Copyright- Surendra Sahu, 2017-2020

Foreword

An entrepreneur is an innovator, job creator, game-changer, leader, disruptor and adventurer. Entrepreneurs think out of the box, they love problem solving and love making customers happy. It is well known that ninety percent of new enterprises or start-ups fail. Can entrepreneurship be taught or it can be learned? Do entrepreneurs have some special qualities that make them successful? How to become a successful entrepreneur? Does an entrepreneur have to be a risk-taker? The book tries to answer all these questions under topics conveniently classified.

Surendra Sahu

Contents

1. Introduction..5-7
2. Identifying Business Opportunity....................9-10
3. Steps of Entrepreneurship............................10-12
4. Strategic Decision making for Entrepreneurs..12-13

5. Customers & Market....................................13-16

6. Product development plan...........................16-17

7. Business Model and Plan..............................17-20

8. Employees..21-22

9. Managing growth...22-25

10. Failure..29-30

11. Dealing with entrepreneurial stress............30-31

12. Money and Returns..31

13. Qualities of an Entrepreneur......................31-41

14. Success 41-44

15. Vision...44

16. Work..44-45

17. Advice from successful entrepreneurs......45-48

A GUIDE TO ENTREPRENEURSHIP

1. Introduction

   The term entrepreneurship is derived from the French word "entreprendre" which means to " undertake". Thus the entrepreneur is someone who undertakes to do something which may result in a product or service. It is to become an entrepreneur but difficult to become a successful entrepreneur who can run his unit for reasonable period of time and keep on making profits in the long run although losses for al limited period of time is acceptable. In the following pages we will study the history , growth and hardships faced some of the well-known companies both Indian and international .Hopefully we can learn some lessons from their stories and the aspiring entrepreneur can derive his own lessons.

   The entrepreneur must be willing to be misunderstood for long periods of time. -Jeff Bozos(founder of Amazon).

   Don't let social media fool you. Entrepreneurship is not as glamorous as it seems, you will be broke, depressed and ready to quit at times... don't quit.

   Entrepreneurship cannot be taught. The individual must feel an inner need to take this up.

   An entrepreneur is someone who has a vision for something and a want to create.

   Put out your ideas to the world. Your thoughts will be accepted by others if they are viable.

You may have great ideas, but the key factor for your success is the execution.

All entrepreneurship is trial and error. Because you cannot exactly ascertain what the customer needs or likes.

Focus on success and do learn from the failures.

Entrepreneurs always find a way.

There is no learning without trying lots of ideas and failing lots of times.

Entrepreneur is someone who jumps off a cliff and builds a plane on the way down.

Success and profitability are outcomes of focusing on customers and employees and not objectives.

Entrepreneurship is a lot like athletics. You need to practice and train. Read books. Listen to podcasts of successful entrepreneurs. Look for role models /mentors. One learns by doing and not by understanding the theory of how to do it.

Being a true entrepreneur is like being an elite athlete. It is not the "cheat days" and "rest days" that make it. It is the hard work. The persistence. The effort. The drive. The commitment. It is about the mastery.

Successful entrepreneurs are givers and not takers of positive energy.

If you want to do it, do it now.

An entrepreneur is someone who has a vision for something and a want to create.

An entrepreneur goes to bed thinking about his business and wakes up thinking about the business.

Entrepreneurship in not about proving someone wrong by proving oneself right.

Entrepreneur is a word that means you are going to work, take risk, be disappointed. It is a big commitment.

Entrepreneurs love the challenge. It is not about just making money.

A true entrepreneur is not a dreamer but a doer.

Entrepreneur is a word that means you are going to work, take risk, be disappointed. It is a big commitment.

An entrepreneur is someone who has a vision for something, and a want to create.

You need to try enough things and fail.

Being an entrepreneur means working 80 hours a week (for a few years) to avoid working a lifetime for someone else.

Solve a real problem. You don't start a company because you want to be an entrepreneur or the fame and glory that comes with it. You become an entrepreneur to solve a real problem.

Entrepreneurship is the ability to endure. Chaos happens. If you do not have blinding guiding light, you will fall apart.

Entrepreneurs sacrifice a lot to accomplish their goals. This sacrifice includes sleep. We get only limited time in a day and for most entrepreneurs, this is not enough.

You must take the right decision at the right time to produce the right results.

You will make many mistakes. Do not be afraid of the. The main point is to learn from them and correct your strategy.

Entrepreneurs are great at dealing with uncertainty and also very good at minimizing risk. That is the classic great entrepreneur.

Entrepreneurship cannot be taught. The individual must feel an inner need to take this up.

Put out your ideas to the world. Your thoughts will be accepted by others if they are viable.

You may have great ideas, but the key factor for your success is the execution.

All entrepreneurship is trial and error. Because you cannot exactly ascertain what the customer needs or likes.

Focus on success and do learn from the failures.

There is no learning without trying lots of ideas and failing lots of times.

Success and profitability are outcomes of focusing on customers and employees and not objectives.

Don't start a company unless you are obsessed with the product or service and something you love.

You must know what is going on in your company.

Why entrepreneurship?

The following are the reasons why one takes up entrepreneurship.

a. Making Money: How much money you earn is considered a measure of one's success.
b. Control: You can be your own boss when you become an entrepreneur.
c. To Create: You can create a product or service which can be great personal satisfaction.
d. To help: You can help others by providing a needed a product or service which may impact healthcare or education or job creation.

Why not Entrepreneurship?

People do not venture into entrepreneurship due to the following reasons.

a. Risk: Entrepreneurship involves risk of finance and time.
b. Fear of failure: Entrepreneurship is accompanied by failures. Not all your ideas will succeed.
c. Opportunity cost: It is the income you lose which you would have earned if you did not indulge in entrepreneurship.
d. Ridicule: It you fail in your enterprise, other people ridicule you.
e. Peer pressure: Friends often advise not to start an enterprise.

f. Family influence: Family is concerned about your financial well-being and may advise you against starting an enterprise and look for a job of steady income.

When is the right time to start an enterprise?

Although many people start an enterprise in their thirties or forties, it is better start in one's twenties as one does not have a family in that period and less responsibilities which makes it easier for him to take risks.

2. Identifying Business Opportunity

In order to identify a business opportunity one needs to ask the following questions:
1. What is the problem you propose to solve?
2. How do you propose to solve it?
3. What is the potential market impact?
4. What is the customer "pain" you are attempting to address?
5. What is the market doing now to address this problem?

3. Steps of entrepreneurship

Entrepreneurship consists of following steps:
a. Opportunity recognition: It is the identification of a new technology product or a service to fulfill a unsatisfied need of customers. It removes the pains of the customers or results in gains to the customer.
b. Pursuit of opportunity: Once an opportunity is recognized it is necessary to pursue this opportunity to a money-making process. For

this one requires people, organization, resources and capital. One has to identify one's customers.
c. Entrepreneurship is converting a vision into a product or service through strategy and execution. Through this process an idea is converted into an opportunity.
d. Risk reduction: Entrepreneur tries to reduce risk at every step.
e. Hypothesis testing and experimentation: It is for the entrepreneur to create value of the customer. The entrepreneur has to figure out what he wants to do with the resources available to him. Thus entrepreneurship is essentially a search process and experimentation of the idea of the entrepreneur.
f. Before investing the entrepreneur has to figure out about the market size and the target customers.
g. Market creation: Market can be created through social networking sites such as facebook, twitter, google plus and linked-in and giving advertisement on google and creating website through wordpress.com.
h. Business model canvas: The entrepreneur has to prepare a business model rather than a business plan to succeed.

A Business Model describes the rationale of how an organization creates, delivers, and captures value. A typical business model will consist of following elements.

1. Key Activities
2. Key Resources
3. Value Proposition
4. Customer Relationships.
5. Channels
6. Customer Segments
   Defines the different groups of people or organisation an enterprise aims to serve separate segments if:
   - Needs require and justify distinct offers.
   - Reached through different distribution channels.
   - Requires different types of relationships.
   - Have substantially different profitabilities.
   - Are willing to pay for different aspects.
7. Partners
8. Cost structure
9. Revenue Streams
   Strategies for business Model:
   1. Create uncontested marketplace.
   2. Make the competition irrelevant.
   3. Create and capture new demand.
   4. Break the value-cost trade-off.
   5. Align the whole system of a firm's activities in pursuit of differentiation and low cost.

4. Strategic Decision Making for Entrepreneurs

Environment of entrepreneur is uniquely challenging. Entrepreneurs have to take quick and high-risk decisions with incomplete information in a dynamic market. Some of the factors to be kept in mind are:

    a. Cognition: It is the selection of specific course of action that is supposed to bring a desired result.

    b. Choice: Where alternatives exist, how does choose one. Exact outcomes are often unknown.

    c. How to reduce uncertainty?

    d. Consider what is the current market situation but also what direction it is taking.

    e. What are the revenue and profit goals?

    f. What market share you want to capture and what is the competitive advantage of your product?

Strategic decisions involve critical analysis, resource investment and company commitment. It involves the planning of actions in uncertain and unpredictable future. It can result in substantial gains or losses.

5. Customers & Market:

The purpose of a business is to create a customer who creates customers.

Exploring Real Market Needs

    To create a successful new company you need to introduce a product or service that satisfies customer needs in a better way than competitors, and a t a price that is greater than the cost of creating and delivering that product or service. How to identify a real customer need?

Best clue is a customer complaint.

Satisfying Real Market Needs
The entrepreneur needs to ask the following questions.
  a. Why would customer use my product?
  b. What is the best way to customer needs?
  c. What features to incorporate in the product or service; size, weight, durability etc.)
  d. Why does my product fit customer needs better than those of current and future competitors?
  e. What price should I charge?

Beware of overdesigning your product to the point that the price is beyond your customer.

Keep production costs manageable and volume appropriately high. Gather information about competitors and their products. Talk to friends, family and potential customers to get feedback.

To be successful at entrepreneurship, one also has to understand how to market and sell new products and services.

Success and profits depend on pricing right.

Beware of under pricing your product which may be perceived to be of low quality.

One must truly understand the needs of one's customers.

Treat your customers like they own you. Because they do.

You have to adjust to the reality. You have to change your mind if required.

The market only cares about the product and not for the promoters of the business.

You must differentiate your product or service in the market as there many competitors.

Your most unhappy customers are your greatest source of learning.

In this one has to ask the following questions.
- Who are the customers
- What are their problems
- Confirm/revise your assumptions about the customer.
- Types of customers:
  - Needs and wants
  - Day in the life of the customer
  - Return on Investment (ROI) for the customer.
  - Minimum and desired features.
  - NEEDS+ Sales+ Marketing=Buying

Also the following issues have to be addressed:

1. Whether to launch a Beta product and improve it further depending upon customer feedback or a fully developed product.
2. Pricing: Most entrepreneurs are tempted to price their product way below their competitors. Low price may be seen as indicative of low quality. It is recommended to keep the price of the product 10 to 20 per cent cheaper than the competition.
3. Promotion

- Understanding customer needs and wants is core to your success.
- Market planning is central to entering markets and sustaining success.
- New Competitors are ever present.

6. Sales Forecasting
    - Plan your business.
        - How much to sell?
        - How much inventory to buy+
        - How many people to hire?
        - Convince investors and lenders.
        - Financial projections for the future.
        - Improve your business.
            - Trends in revenues.
            - How can we improve profitability?

7. Product Development Plan
    a. How the testing of the prototype will be done by independent testers?
        - What are its weak points?
        - What are the areas of improvement?
        - What level of research and development is required now?
        - If it's a service, how will it be tested with potential customers?
    b. Who is the market?
        - Who is the overall market?
        - What are the markets segments/niches?
        - Within the overall market, can your product penetrate these segments.
        - How big is the market?

- How fast is it growing?
- What are the trends?
- Who else is in the market?-Now and in the future.

c. Production and distribution plan
- PRODUCTION
- How will the product be made?
- Will it be produced in-house or by others?
- At what cost?
- What is the present capacity of the producer?
- What is the break-even point?
- DISTRIBUTION
- What distribution and sales methods will be used?
- How will the product be transported?

d. Staffing and Funding Plans
- STAFFING
- Can the company get or has it already lined up- the necessary skill to operate the business venture.
- What are the skills, experiences etc?
- FUNDING
- How much capital will be needed now?
- What are the major phases of financing?

8. Business Model & Plan

One must change one's business model as the firm continues its operations for the customers' needs and the market conditions change continuously.

One has to be comfortable in changing the business model many times before the actual product launch.

One model which can be used to analyse the plans of your business is as under:

- Revenue model
- Pricing
- Average account size and /or lifetime value.
- sales and distribution model.
- Customer/pipeline list.

The business plan is a plan for creation and management of business with special attention to:

- Marketing plan describing match of strategy and products to current and future markets.
- Operation plan discussing processes.
- Financial plan assessing all costs and financial requirements.

Why write a business plan?

1. Writing forces a person (team) preparing the plan to look at the business in an objective and critical manner.
2. Helps to focus ideas and serves as a feasibility study of the business's chance for success and growth.

3. It serves as an operational tool to define the company's present status and future possibilities.

Business plans are the owner's manual for your company. It provides a tool to plan, track, and adapt your business. It requires significant time write it (and revise to stay relevant).It may have to be revised every few months as market conditions change and you learn.

Objectives of the Business Plan

1. Business plan should be preceded by the Business Model Canvas.
2. It should focus on PSUCF
   P: Problem:
   How many buyers? In number and in dollars or rupees.
   How painful is it to the market.
   How is the problem being dealt with today?
   - Competitors?
   - Substitutes?

   S: Solution

   - Basics of your solution.
   - Basic unique advantage.
   - Define the scale and time-line of the advantage.
- C:Competiton
- F: Financials

B. Writing a Business Plan

There is no uniform format to write business plan. However it may contain 15-20 pages consisting of following information.

1. Company Purpose
2. Problem
   - Describe the pain of the customer.
   - Outline how the customer addresses the issue today.
3. Solution
   - Demonstrate your company's value proposition.
   - Show where your product sits.
   - Provide user cases.
4. Why now?
   - Set up the historical evolution of your category.
   - Define the recent trends that make your solution possible.
5. Market Size
   - Identify the current and expected customers.
   - How many dollars are spent on product like yours.
   - What are the trends(Opportunity and threats)
6. Competition
   - List competitors
   - List competitive advantages
7. Product

- Product line-up.(form factor, functionality, features, architecture, intellectual property)

8. Business Model

- Revenue model

- Pricing

- Average account size and /or lifetime value.

- sales and distribution model.

- Customer/pipeline list.

9. Team:

 - Founders and Management

 - Board of Directors/Board of Advisers

10. Financials

 - Income statement

 - Cash flow statement

 - Balance sheet

11. Executive Summary

Common mistakes in a business plan:

1. Too long.
2. Poor positioning(No validation, your solutions are looking for a problem to solve)
3. Lack of focus

4. Not enough real world market analysis.
5. No business "Cockpit Gauges".
6. Unclear business model
7. Poor or incomplete Competitive analysis.
8. Weak team information.
9. Poorly defined leverage points.
10. Goofy fundamentals that distract.

If after preparing the business plan, profitability does not seem a possibility then the idea may be abandoned and a fresh idea for pursuing a business should be explored.

9. Employees

You cannot do much without people. Find the right people who share your passion.

Hire people smarter than you.

Hire only the best talent.

If want to take a co-founder find someone who has strength in areas other than your own.

Focus on employees and success will follow.

10. Managing Growth

When an enterprise is up and running, it faces the decision whether to grow or not. The following factors have to be kept in mind before deciding whether or not to grow.

Growth can be good or bad. Grow or die is a business myth and is not true. Too much growth before preparation can overwhelm people, processes and controls. The bigger an organization gets, the more complex it becomes. There are more rules, bureaucracy and administrative set-up. The entrepreneurial spirit is lost.

Real-life growth is never linear. It is always zig-zag. It happens in spurts. The businessman has constantly to ask himself the question,. "How do I remain ahead of the pack?" There is a need to constantly improve the product or service to grow.

Growth does not mean more profits. It may cause losses. One has to look at the costs too.

a. For making growth you need strategic focus. Your goal should be two inches wide and two miles deep.
b. One has to work for operational excellence. One has to deliver 99 % defect free and on-time delivery.
c. When you grow, embrace the customer. Listen to your customer till it hurts.
d. One has to be engaged in constant improvement. One has to become better, faster and cheaper.
e. The business has to customer-centric. The customer is more important than the product.

f. The employees should care about the customers and the business like you.
g. Adopt the gas-pedal approach to growth.
h. Growth, if not managed properly, can destroy the organisation's values.
i. Growth requires more people, processes and controls.
j. Growth is expensive. In most cases iot requires cash outlays ahead of growth of income. So think carefully, how much growth you can afford.
k. Growth can push you into a different and more competitive space where you will face bgger, more capitalized players. The game will change.
l. If not managed properly growth can be destructive.

Before undertaking growth one has to ask the following questions:
1. Why should we grow?
2. How will we grow?
3. How much should we grow?
4. How much growth we can afford?
5. Do we have enough people.
6. Do we have the right people.
7. Do we have the right people?
8. Do we have hiring and training processes?
9. Do we have adequate financial controls?
10. How will growth create risks for:
    a. Culture?

- b. Customer service?
- c. Customer experience?
- d. Cash flow?
- e. Supply chains, raw materials and suppliers?
- f. Distribution and delivery?
- g. Financial safety net? How will we mitigate the risks?
- h. Do we have adequate daily information to monitor these risks?
- i. Who will help us monitor, manage and correct such isks or results?
- j. Do we need to pace growth?
- k. Are we ready to grow?
- l. Unknown is scary. Things are uncertain. What do I know? What do I really know? What are the key unknowns I need to know?

11. What are your strengths and weaknesses.
12. What are your personal and business goals.
13. What is your end game.

11. Processes of Growth

    Growth involves the following stages:

    a. Planning:

       Visualise what you structure and infrastructure would look like at bigger stages.

1. What is structure?
   - Your organization chart-by function/job.
   - Size inflection points: 7-9 employees; 20-25 employees; 45-50 employees; 100 employees. A person can manage seven persons working under him.
2. What is Infrastructure?
   - Space needs
   - Furniture, equipment
   - Phones
   - Technology
3. Do you outsource?
   - Payroll processing, accounting, taxes
   - HR benefit processing
   - Manufacturing(Quality control issues)
   - Sales
   - Delivery

b. Priortisation
   1. Personal
      - What am I going to sell?
      - TO WHOM?
      - Why are they going to buy from me? –Is it due to price, quality or the customer experience he has worth my company.
   2. Daily
      - Critical decision—why?
      - Assess the situation and go where you have biggest

impact- fight the biggest fire.
- How do you know? Those issues which affect life, property, brand, reputation, customers, quality or cash.
- Where is the bottleneck?

One entrepreneur likes to emphasise the importance of you product quality in these words: "You do not eat if you do not sell. You don't sell if you do not have a customer. You don't have a customer unless you offer a good product or service.

Another entrepreneur likes to set priories in this way: " Set up 3 or 4 priorities that take precedence over everything else: Manage cash flow; focus on customers and quality service; accelerate revenue growth and all the rest-unless something is on fire- can wait."

- Conduct a daily huddle. A gathering of all employees for a few minutes to

reinforce the organisation's values.
- Performance Metric Transparency: Post daily keep performance metrics to all employees.

3. Processes
   What is a process?
   - Establish checklists as a pilot makes his checklist before the flight takes off.
   - Issue instructions: frame instructions which stipulates the step by step process about how to do something. This is to ensure that 99% of time defect-free and on-time performance delivery is made to the customers.

4. Pacing Growth.
   - Adopt the gas-pedal approach.
   - Have the right people and the right processes in place.
   - Walk before you run.
   - Have clear lines of reporting and authority.

Success for business can be attributed to intense focus.

Businesses do not grow; people do. Provide opportunities for people to grow in your company so that they take the business to the next level.

12. Managing Change

    Changes can occur in the following spheres:
    a. Technology: New technology allows for the expansion of new innovations.
    b. Social and demographic structure
    c. Industry changes.
    d. Political and regulatory factors.

    Direct relationships exist between change and the creation of entrepreneurial opportunities. Identifying the change or gap that makes the opportunity possible is a first step to acting on the opportunity. But for the enterprise to be successful, the opportunity should be objectively evaluated.

13. Failure

    The following are the usual causes of failure of a start-up.
    1. Co-founders fight.
    2. Product /market problems
        a. They cannot build the initial specifications of their product or service.
        b. Little customer understanding
        c. Not truly differentiated.
        d. Trouble establishing the brand.

       e. Too few people buy or use the product.
3. Financial Difficulties
       a. Typically underfunded.
       b. Spend on things that do not strongly influence success.
4. Managerial Problems
       a. Limited team experience.
       b. Scarce team experience
       c. Human resource problems.

Points for consideration for the product or service:

       a. Is it a new product/service idea?
       b. Is it proprietary?
       c. Can it be patented or copyrighted?
       d. Is it unique enough o get a significant head start on the competition before it can be imitated or copied?

Failure could be considered as learning opportunities. They should not discourage you. Vinod Khosla had said, " In small failures you accumulate learnings about what works and what doesn't."

Failure is normal. Learn from them. Never give up.

Failure of start-ups takes place due to improper execution and the inability to find a genuine problem of the masses to solve.

No matter what happens , keep moving towards your desired destination.

An entrepreneur is not someone that wants to be told what to do. An entrepreneur is the one that innovates, improves and find new ways . And that is what they get paid for.

14. Dealing with Entrepreneurial Stress
    The entrepreneur is a highly stressed individual.
    Some of the ways to deal with this stress are.
    Networking: Network with other entrepreneurs.
    Communicating with your employees.
    Vacationing. Take a break every six weeks.
    Exercising.
    Investors

Treat your investors' money more carefully than your own money.

15. Decision Making
    Take quick decisions—and you will make some mistakes, but you need decisions. Many large corporations move too slowly due to bureaucratic red tape.
16. Money and Returns

Never focus on financial returns. Focus on the product or service you have to offer to the world. Financial returns will be a byproduct of your good/service.

Lack of money is also a challenge.

17. Passion

Chase the vision and not the money.

18. Problems

Find a problem of the world to solve and don't just pursue your idea.

Try to find solution to a problem which aligns with your passion.

11. Qualities of an Entrepreneur

> An entrepreneur is a person who organizes and manages any enterprise, especially a business, with considerable initiative and risk.

>> An entrepreneur is an independent individual intensely committed and determined to persevere and works very hard.

> An entrepreneur is someone who can identify a right idea which fulfills the aspirations of the public and can execute

> An entrepreneur must have the emotional intelligence to be successful. He should be able to gauge how others feel.

> An entrepreneur must learn to differentiate himself from his business.
> An entrepreneur must learn to differentiate himself from his business.
> Anxiety and feelings of loneliness kills more entrepreneurs than lack of funding.
> Any one who has right skills and right temperament and who can sell his or her skills can be an entrepreneur.
> ■■
> Be a continuous learner.

Be better than your competition; get business on merits.

Be passionate about the thing you do.

Be passionate about the thing you do. Believe in your idea. Don't go by others' advice or opinions.
Borrow ideas shamelessly, repackage, re-apply and revise to meet Successful entrepreneurs satisfy customer needs better, faster and/or cheaper than their competitors. Follow the money-cash is king.
Build honest, trusting and transparent relations.
Continue learning.
■■■
Create a routine.

Customers know best what they need.
■■■
Develop strong habits.

Do something useful. Adapt to the changing circumstances and do the very best at that point of time.
■■■
Do something useful. Adapt to the changing circumstances and do the very best at that point of time.

> Don't focus only on earning money. Try to delight the customer with an amazing product. Money will come as a by-product.
> Don't listen to others' advice. Especially the uncalled for ones. Go by your gut feelings.
> Encourage your team to provide solutions not problems.

Entrepreneurs are clever risk mitigators.

Entrepreneurs are willing to live abnormal lives.

Entrepreneurs average 3.8 failures before final success. What sets the successful ones apart is their amazing persistence.

Entrepreneurs cannot help it. They jusat know with every ounce in their being that they are destined for greater things in life.

Entrepreneurs don't take big risks but test ideas quickly by taking small risks.
....
Entrepreneurs focus on constant improvement.

Entrepreneurs focus on what they have.

Entrepreneurs get into business with potential customers and learn from doing.
....
Entrepreneurs give a minimum viable product.

Entrepreneurs learn as they go and iterate.

Entrepreneurs listen to their gut instinct and act accordingly. They may listen to others.
....
Entrepreneurs see the inevitable and advance the future.

Entrepreneurs take calculated risks. It is like an arranged marriage. You know some things about the girl and her family but not quite fully.

Entrepreneurship is throwing yourself off a cliff and assembling an airplane on the way down.-Reid Hoffman , cofounder of Linked in.

Focus less on profit but on relationships.
■■

Give a head-start to tomorrow today. List out two priorities today night which you must complete tomorrow.

Happy and highly engaged employees result in superior performance which leads to happy customers and which brings in the dollars.
■■

He burns with the competitive desire to excel.

He has a drive to achieve.

He has a great tolerance for ambiguity and is comfortable with changes.

He has a high energy level.

He has a tolerance for failure.

He has an internal locus of control and believes that his success is due to his efforts and not due to luck or external factors.

He is a confident optimist who strives for integrity.

He is a visionary.

He is creative and innovative.

He is self confident .

He likes to be independent.

He must be a learner for life .

He must be emotionally mature and highly motivated.

He must keep his overheads low as possible.
■■

He must use the available gadgets for productivity and efficiency.
■■■■■■■■■■■■■■■■■■■■■■■■■■■■■■■■■■■■■■■

He seeks feedback from his customers.

He should be able to learn rapidly based on market feedback.

> He should be able to work with investors.
> He should be free from anxiety and feeling loneliness. Such feelings kill more entrepreneurs rather than lack of funds.
> He takes calculated risks.
> He takes initiative and owns responsibility.
> He takes up team building.
> He tries hire people who are better than him or who fill up the skill-set which he does not possess.
> He uses failure as a learning tool.

If you enjoy doing something, then that is the right job for you.

If you enjoy doing something, then that is the right job for you.

In order to be successful you need to experiment. In the words of Michael Dell, "Experiment, test, go fats, fail fast. You learn tent times faster by doing it, rather than thinking about it."

> It is better that the entrepreneur maximizes his learning early in his career.
> It is good to build up connections. This may help in future.

Keep the morning for the toughest projects.

Listen to your customers.
Make the product or service you make an object of desire for the customer. Make it compelling so that customer cannot but buy it.
Make your people contribute to your company.

Not all successful entrepreneurs came from industrial families but became successful by pursuing their dreams, passions and making the best use of the situation.

One makes money in an enterprise by adding value to the people, your customers.

■■

Refresh themselves with quality family time.

Schedule time for revenue generating activities.

Segregate each day for separate business activity.

Successful entrepreneurs are action oriented. They keep working until they get it right for their customers. Successful entrepreneurs take small steps, not big risks, and test options. They learn from their experience when they face the unknown and uncertainty.

Take a vow of poverty in the initial few years of of existence of your enterprise.

Take regular breaks from your work to gain focus.

The entrepreneur has to face failures and setbacks but must realign his strategy to get back into business.

The entrepreneur has to use his money judiciously and should not use the profits of the company for private purposes for the first three years of operation of the company.

The entrepreneur must be hungry for knowledge for it empowers.

■■

The entrepreneur must have a deep knowledge of the product or service which he thinks of providing to customers.

The entrepreneur must love what he does. If not, he is bound to give in the face of failure. But if loves his work he is likely to persevere till he gets success.
The entrepreneur should build his strength and stamina.

The entrepreneur should have extraordinary energy, grit and self drive.

The entrepreneur should have fun; enjoy doing what he does; should carry fear of losing a lot of things(such as money, reputation) and dream big.

The entrepreneur should never be emotional but be always strategic.

The job of an entrepreneur is the creation of knowledge.
The journey of entrepreneurship is to discover one's strengths, weaknesses, susceptibilities and possibilities.

The journey of the entrepreneur is rigorous. It requires extraordinary grit, energy and self-drive. You have to deliver.

The journey of the entrepreneur is rigorous. It requires extraordinary grit, energy and self-drive. You have to deliver.

There are cynics all around. An entrepreneur stays positive.

They are good with people. People like doing business with nice people need employees like working with nice people.

They do not take high risks.

They find needs that many customers have. Sometimes you may give them a product or service they don't know they have a need of.

They listen to their customers. They are not stubborn, defensive or rigid.

■■■

They take small bets and get engaged with the customers.

They work in and learn a business before starting a similar business.

To be successful you need a good product that meets customer needs for a fair price.

■■■

To me, entrepreneurship means being able to create a life for you where you are in control and you call the shots. -Toni Panosian

Track their progress.

Work less to achieve more. Work for ninety minutes and take ten minutes break. Take a day off in a week to rejuvenate. Work for six weeks and take one week break.

■■■

Workout and meditate.

You do not need a unique product or service but you have to better listen to your customer and help your customer to meet their needs.

You need to give your customers great service. You should be comfortable giving up job security.

■■■

You should be comfortable giving up job security.

■■■

Innovation

It is the entire process by which an organization generates creative new technological ideas(invention) and converts them into novel, useful and viable commercial products, services and business processes for (potential) economic value. Other definitions of innovation are:

a. The act of introducing something new.
b. A new idea, method or device.
c. The successful exploitation of new ideas.
d. Change that creates a new dimension of performance.

19. Risk taking

Successful entrepreneurs need not take high risks. In fact they take low risk. Entrepreneurs tend to accept risks, resist norms and are less predictable in decision making. They see things differently than others Different types of risk which exist are: financial, personal safety and ethical. If you are not willing to take risk, you cannot grow. If you cannot grow, you cannot be your best.

How does an entrepreneur prevent himself from overgeneralization? The following may be adopted.

a. Actively search for information.
b. Define assumptions.
c. Consider alternatives.
d. Estimate the consequences.
e. Work as a team.
f. Ask for advice.

How to zero on a product or service which customers want and are willing to pay.?The following steps may be followed.

    a. Build(Turn ideas into products)
    b. Measure(See how customers respond to your product)
    c. Learn(Learn from customer feedback and persevere to give a product to the customer which delights him)
    d. And the cycle goes on.

It is important for entrepreneurs and (and for aspiring entrepreneurs) to assess risk and thereby improve their decision-making.

The entrepreneur must have the capacity to take risks.

Take calculated risks. Do not be rash or suicidal in your decisions. Venture into an area about which you know- its market, competitors etc.

Everyone can tell you the risk. An entrepreneur can see the reward.

A real entrepreneur has no safety net under him.

A real entrepreneur has no safety net beneath him.

20. Success

It is easy to establish an enterprise but difficult to survive and grow. The outside environment may not be favourable to your enterprise. You may face failure in your ideas and efforts. The following ideas will help you to succeed in your venture.

1. Be totally committed to make your enterprise work. Make all-out efforts. You have to tell yourself, "I have to do."
2. Before you enter a field, have some work experience in that field which will give you a good idea about processes and market conditions
3. Brand is about consistency and a brand is trusted. Don't release a beta version to the market if you are still working to better it. Doing so may harm your reputation.
4. Build processes into your enterprise.
5. Business is often unpredictable. Your assumptions about the customer and market may be proven wrong.
6. Connect market opportunity with the right product.
7. Don't focus on reducing cost only to stay in the market. Doing so will reduce your profits. Instead concentrate on Research and Development and bringing new products.
8. Don't venture into high-risk areas. Most successful start-ups begin with low risks.
9. Entrepreneurship is a demanding experience and it will require your total involvement and employment of your entire skill-set.
10. For a new enterprise to succeed and survive it is not enough if you are slightly better than existing enterprises. You need to be a lot better than you competitors.

11. Fund raising is always difficult. When you start out rely on your own savings and support from friends and relatives.
12. Hire people not to show off but as per actual needs.
13. If you have to have a partner, identify your strengths and weaknesses. Choose a partner who can complement your skill-set.
14. In order that people may join you, you have to sell your vision them.
15. In to-day's competitive market you need to listen to the customer.
16. It is good to attend conferences and attend classes or other social get-together for these will give you networking opportunities which may prove beneficial in your career.
17. It is good to learn from the entrepreneurs who have been successful in your field and take advice from them.
18. Learn to say "No" to many things. If it is not relevant to your company don't involve yourself.
19. Make your borrowings as low as possible for interest burdens can be killing.
20. Market is a battle field. Thus thorough knowledge of the market is essential.
21. Once you are convinced of your business model, approach angel investors or High Net Worth Individuals for financing your project.

22. One has to many times reinvent oneself many time during one's life.
23. Success starts with passion.
24. You are bound to face failure on many fronts. If you face repeated failures what do you do? Remember failure is the fertilizer for success. One has to learn lessons from the failures and move on.
■■■■■■■■■■■■■■■■■■■■■■■■■■■■■■■■■■■
25. You have to earn a spot in the market to survive.
26. You need to be talented in your field.
27. You need to constantly innovate to remain in business.
28. Your family may not always support you in your ventures. It is good to get a support group to achieve some mental balance.

It may take time to achieve the desired level of success. It is important not to lose faith in oneself.

Leverage your strengths.

Lack of knowledge is really a challenge to an entrepreneur. So try to know as much as possible of the areas of your business operations.

21. Vision

Have a vision for your business.

Purpose is more important than vision. Vision needs to change s time passes on or context changes.

22. Work

As an entrepreneur figure out what you have to do. You are not a manager with a fixed job description.

You have to work hard, perhaps eighteen hours a day.

Lack of time is also a challenge. Devote yourself to the tasks that will bring maximum results for your business.

Work for your happiness/

Give your best. Don't give up. Think success is the only adoption.

Set a goal- don't stop until you achieve it.

For great achievements inspiration is more important than financial returns.

Set a deadline for accepting setback, failure, loss—at least emotionally. This acceptance is crucial—and so is the deadline. My deadline is 48 hours.

23. Advice from successful entrepreneurs
    a. Do something important. -Elon Musk
    b. Never give up. -Elon Musk
    c. Take a risk. -Elon Musk
    d. Really like what you do. -Elon Musk
    e. Don't listen to the little man. -Elon Musk
    f. Have a great product. -Elon Musk
    g. Attract great people. -Elon Musk
    h. Work super hard. -Elon Musk
    i. Look for problem solvers. -Elon Musk
    j. Most people give up just when they are about to achieve success.

k. Howard Schultz was turned down by banks 242 times before he went on to found Starbucks, the American chain of coffee shops.
l. Don't aim to get materialistic things, aim to make a change. Then you will succeed.
m. Create a routine and try to follow it daily.
n. Schedule time for revenue generating activities. Track their progress.
o. Keep on learning continuously.
p. Segregate each day for separate business activity.

A company is a group of people. You as an owner have to listen to your people and praise them so that feel a sense of ownership for the companies they are leading.- Richard Branson, founder of Virgin Group of Companies

q. A good entrepreneur is not rigid in his ideas He changes his mind a lot with new points of view, new information, new ideas, contradictions and challenges.
r. A players hire A people.-Guy Kawasaki
s. Entrepreneurship is living a few years of life like most people won't, so that, you can spend the rest of your life like most people can't.-Unknown
t. Be stubborn on vision and flexible on details.- Jeff Bozos, founder of amazon.com
u. Biggest challenges get the best work from people.- Guy Kawasaki
v. Do something you are passionate about. If you don't succeed still you will engage in it. And eventually you may achieve success.-Steve Jobs
w. Don't go full hog into the business. Maintain a full time income while you build a business. Work in a

great company and a start-up to learn the tricks of the trade.
x. Don't set goals. If these are not achieved it induces stress. Without goals you may explore new territory. You will learn unexpected things and you'll end up in surprising places.
y. Don't wait for the perfect product to launch. Get out, go to market, learn and move on.
z. Don't whine about your mistakes, learn from them.-Bill Gates
aa. Focus on what you do, rewards will follow.
bb. Give employees freedom to make mistakes. For we learn through our mistakes.
cc. Go with your gut feeling to decide on your business ventures.-Richard Branson
dd. Groups should consists of 5 to 7 people. Larger teams are inefficient.- Jeff Bozos, founder of amazon.com
ee. Have a proper work-life balance. Leave office at 5. 30 pm and devote time to your family.
ff. Hire people better than you
gg. Hire people who have different strengths than yours and not similar people as yourself. -Guy Kawasaki
hh. It is important to be humble.
ii. Life is not fair, get used to it.-Bill Gates
jj. Never stop experimenting.- Jeff Bozos, founder of amazon.com
kk. People are your most important assets.
ll. Play for the long haul. Don't expect quick rewards.
mm. Provide the strongest guarantee you can for your product and services.

nn. Real CEOs can demonstrate themselves. -Guy Kawasaki
oo. Real entrepreneurs are able to present a real product to the market. -Guy Kawasaki
pp. Seek out negative feedback. Negative constructive feedback will refine your ideas.
qq. Success is 99 per cent failures and one per cent what you learn from these failures. -Soichiro Honda, founder of Honda Motors
rr. Surround yourself with people who call a spade a spade.
ss. Take as little funding as possible at the beginning.
tt. Take lots of small steps to reach a great future.-Bill Graham
uu. The entrepreneur must have something on his worry plate every day.-A US Entrepreneur
vv. The world will expect you to accomplish something before you feel good about yourself.-Bill Gates
ww. Entrepreneurship is living a few years of life like most people won't, so that you can spend the rest of your life like most people can't.-Unknown
xx. Thus there is no sure shot way to success for the entrepreneur. One has to experiment with low risks and then learn from failures until one becomes successful.To achieve start-up success one has to fail over and over again until one learns what you need to succeed.You need to be unique and valuable.23. .Further Guidance for EntrepreneursEntrepreneurship is a lot like athletics. You need to practice and train. Read books. Listen to podcasts of successful entrepreneurs. Look for role models /mentors. One

learns by doing and not by understanding the theory of how to do it. Being a true entrepreneur is like being an elite athlete. It is not the "cheat days" and "rest days" that make it. It is the hard work. The persistence. The effort. The drive. The commitment. It is about the mastery. Successful entrepreneurs are givers and not takers of positive energy.

yy. A doer and not a dreamer
■■■■■■■■■■■■■■■■■■■■■■■■■■■■■■■■■■■■■■■

www.ingramcontent.com/pod-product-compliance
Lightning Source LLC
Chambersburg PA
CBHW030515220526
45464CB00006B/2810